The Alpha Male's Guide to Satisfying Women

The 3 F's to Keep Women Happy

© 2017

Table of Contents

Introduction

You're an alpha male, right? Hopefully if you're reading this book. At the very least you want to be an alpha male, but that's not all you want. Is it? So you're here because you want to satisfy women, and you want to do it the right way. Relationships can be hard, and I'm not going to tell you to bring your girlfriends flowers every day. You don't have to go out of your way to recite a romantic poem over a bed of roses to keep a woman. There are three simple rules, the three simple F's that you have to do to keep any woman happy and satisfied. That's what we all want, right? To keep a woman happy enough to stay by our side.

The 3 F's

These are pretty crude, but they're also pretty simple. These three F's will help you to do everything you need to fully satisfy and keep a woman. They'll all be explained in later chapters too! Favor her. Feed her. Fuck her. That's the three F's to keeping any woman happy. It may sound a bit odd, but really think about it.

Women love when you show that you care about them or 'favor' them above others. A woman also loves when you cook her food and put effort into her well-being. A woman loves sex just as much as you do, and a relationship that isn't satisfying in the bedroom for both of you isn't one that will last.
That's why the 3 F's really do work! In this book we'll go a little more in depth on what the 3 F's mean and what else you can do to keep women happy and satisfied that tie into these three prominent rules.

Being an Alpha Male

If you're here, you're probably already an alpha. Alphas are men that always know what they want and how to get their way, but there's more to. You have to fight against the normal alpha stereotype as well as make sure that you have everything you need to get started with this book. So many people think that to be an alpha male they have to be domineering, loud, and imposing. This isn't the case. You can be an alpha male as well as a gentlemen, and it is this type of alpha male that will be able to keep women happy. In this chapter you'll learn what it means to be a good alpha male.

Being Direct

No this doesn't mean just talking up to a woman and telling her to get into bed with you. It doesn't mean just demanding free things, but it does mean that you need to speak about what you want. This is the first thing that you should know is that to be an alpha male you should be willing to go after what you want, and that's a good thing.

As an alpha you have to know people and what they do, but you also need to know yourself as an alpha too. You need to be honest, and you need to own up to your intentions and be direct and honest with what you want from everything that you do. Don't apologize for going after what you want and being assertive in your everyday life. This doesn't mean that you need to be a jackass to everyone. Just continue to do what is best for you and those you care about, being direct about how you get to what you want.

So ask yourself a series of questions. Do you just want to have sex with her? Do you want to enjoy a relationship with her? Do you just want to get to know her? Do you want to impress her? Do you want to have her addicted to you and completely satisfy her? Maybe it's something a little simpler than that, and its okay to start simple. Every relationship starts with a hello after all.

Maybe you want to go up and talk to a woman. You don't try to mask your intentions if you're an alpha male. You'll need to be direct and start the conversation. She doesn't want you to act like you aren't interested. Make direct eye contact with her after walking up to her directly. Don't forget to smile and be simple with it. You always want to start with being polite. Women aren't going to respond to being treated poorly, but they will respond to this type of assertiveness.

Project Confidence

This is all about your stride and your attitude, and it'll go a long ways. Saunter up to someone and walk with confidence. Women love when a man is confidence, and it makes you feel like you have control of yourself, your future, and your emotions. This will show that you have control of a situation as well.

One way to project confidence is to be committed to talking to her or doing whatever you want to do. If you don't commit, bail early, or hesitate then you don't show confidence. Women want to be with someone that has control over themselves and commit to someone. No one wants a man that has commitment issues, and that extends far past just committing to a relationship. Below you'll find a few ways to project confidence.

- **Dressing Properly:** Dress to impress so that you can project confidence. A clean appearance is good, but it's okay to be a little scruffy as well. You need to dress how you like and feel comfortable in however you dress. Don't get those old dirty clothing, and don't chose ill-fitting clothing either.

  Chose something that fits your body type and where you're going. It doesn't matter if you chose that black t-shirt with jeans or a button-up with slacks. What matters is that you are comfortable with it as well as making sure that it's clean, fits you, and it's without stains. That will make all of the difference, and you'd be surprised how many men actually wear clothing that doesn't fit their body type if you just glance around you.

- **Adaptability:** Be adaptable but don't settle. Not everything is going to go your ways, but you're an alpha male. That means you can't' seem like you're throwing a tantrum. No one wants to be with someone that gripes and complains. It will keep you from appearing attractive. If things don't go your way, make the best of the situation. Don't let yourself be bothered, but don't feel like you have to settle either. If the food isn't good, send it back.

If you don't like the drink, order another one. So what if the waiter brought you something that barely passes as a good margarita with your tacos on a good day?

What matters is that you don't scoff or treat them poorly. What matters is that you just send it back and don't get to upset. If you don't like the people that are around, then take her somewhere else. So what if there are obnoxious people at the beach? Just take her to somewhere a little more private.

- **Don't Back Down:** Don't back down in the face of disappointment. If you show here that you're disappointed and dismayed, it doesn't seem like you're in control of the situation. So what if you had to send that margarita back? Does that mean you should just choose not to drink? No you can order a beer or something else. If it's too bad you can tell her you don't want her to settle for second best and chose to pay for your drinks and go somewhere else so that you can have the drinks that you deserve. You need to be adaptable as an alpha male because you need to understand that there are more than one way to get what you want. Look at all of the options you have available to you with a level head, and then adjust your plans accordingly.

- **Stand Up:** Stand up for yourself but don't be aggressive about it. Standing up for yourself while being calm and collected is both sexy and appealing, showing you're a leader. As an alpha male you have to expect people to challenge you from time to time, and you should never be scared of these challenges. Just embrace them with a cool and collected demeanor. Make sure that you never let that easy going confidence and smile fade in the face of challenges.

Become a Leader

An alpha leads his pack, and eve if you don't lead a pack you were still born to lead. You have to remember that this is important to being an alpha. To be an alpha you need to have leadership. When you approach a woman directly, you'll want to lead the interaction. This doesn't mean that you should keep her from talking. It just means that you need to take things into your own hands, and don't wait for her to send your signals or to interpret signs.

Are you having a conversation with someone and it's not going where you want it to? There's an easy solution to that! Steer the conversation where you want it to go. For example, if you want to have an emotional relationship then you'll need to open up first. In a long term relationship this is applicable as well. You need to continue to engage in emotional honesty when you're with someone if you want to make sure that your girlfriend continues as well. You have to not only build a rapport but you need to maintain a rapport as an alpha male as well. Below you'll find a few ways to steer the conversation.

- Change the subject if you feel that it's petering off.
- Make a joke if you feel the situation is to tense.
- Use emotions, especially sad ones, to your interactions so that you can use it as a way to have connection with her.
- Gentle touches will help to go a long ways. Put your hand

on her shoulder, grab her hand, or even just lean in a little closer.

- Suggest a scene change if you feel you need to. You can always go for a walk for example.

Body Language

It's more than just about the clothes that you wear. It's about what your body is saying to those around you, especially the woman that you're trying to satisfy. Body language is also important for an alpha male, and if you don't have strong and confident body language then you can't be considered an alpha.

There are some things that are just unbecoming of an alpha male. You can't have your shoulders slumped or head bowed. While this is okay from time to time in a relationship, you cannot make it a regular affair.

If you do, then your woman will lose confidence in the fact that you can take care of them and provide for them. Below you'll find a few ways to project good body language.

- Keep your head up high.
- Make eye contact with who you're talking to.
- Keep your shoulders squared.
- Keep your feet shoulder length apart.
- Don't lock your knees in place.
- Sit up straight, but don't be rigid.
- Walk slowly and take balanced steps.
- When you sit down, do so straight but also comfortably.
- Exposing your torso means you aren't afraid of confrontation.

An Alpha Voice

You may be stuck with the voice that you were born with, but there's more to it than just your normal every day voice. There is tone inflection that you need to express as well, and your voice will change some depending on your mood and if you're aroused. This should be simple but sometimes you need to remind yourself. An alpha male will always speak like an alpha male.

This means that you don't rush your words. You are slow and deliberate, thinking about each one. Remember that once you say something you can't take it back, and your words are like your armor as well as your weapon. Make sure that your voice isn't high or tense when you're speaking. Here are some tips for making your voice that of an alpha males.

- Lower your voice at the end of your sentences when you're trying to sound husky.
- Make sure to annunciate your words so that you're clearly heard.
- Be direct when you're talking. Don't turn your head while talking to someone.
- Talk slowly so that you don't try to rush your words.

Overall Personality

Many people think that an alpha male has to compete with other men, but if you're trying, then you aren't a real alpha male. Real alpha males don't compete with other men because they're confident in their ability and personality. Alpha males aren't competitive. They're actually meant to be cooperative because they have the social skills for it. If someone insults you, don't insult them back. Your social skills are better than that. Instead, just introduce yourself with a smile, tell him it was funny, and even offer to shake his hand. This will re-assert your dominance without being aggressive.

The 1st F: Favor Her

You've already determined that you're an alpha, so let's get down to business. This is the first F, and it's the first thing you need to do to keep a woman completely satisfied. It's time to focus on the girl you want to keep happy if you really want to keep her. You have to favor her. That's an odd phrase, so you might have a few questions. What does that mean? What does it mean to favor someone? It can't just be giving them things, and it isn't. It's so much more than that.

You need to go the extra mile for your girl if you want to completely satisfy her. It's your effort that really makes all of the difference, and you'll just need to show her that you're putting in the effort. You have to try, and that effort is really going to make all of the difference. You need to become a master at getting things done for her. You need to try to make her life easier, and make sure that her experience with you isn't one that she's likely to forget. You want to have it where your woman's wants to stay your woman. She wants to spend the rest of her life with you because you add to it.

Why would a girl want to be with someone that doesn't make them feel like they're on top of the world? No one wants to be around someone that makes them feel that they're just like the countless other women out there. You make her feel special, and you need to treat her like she is special. There isn't a better way to say this. You have to learn what your girlfriend wants and needs in her life.

Does she need help with de-stressing after work? Does she need you to be a regular thing in her life? Does she want you to give her space because she likes alone time? Does she have a hard time cooking? Figure it out so you know what you can offer her. This effort to help enrich her life will show that you care about her more than just the average girl passing through.

This doesn't mean that you need to bend over backwards and try to give her the world. You don't have to jump at every request like a well-trained dog, and if you try to become that type of person it will backfire on you. Women want a man that has a strong character, strong boundaries, and yet is still confidently seeing them as something worth going the extra mile for. Don't become her doormat, became an efficient lover that pays attention to her needs outside of the bedroom as well.

Being More Thoughtful

There are many simple ways to help you be a little more thoughtful in your relationship. Romance doesn't need to be overly complicated, so try to look for the simple things that can make her happy. There's a beauty in doing something simple and thoughtful. Below you'll find a few ways to be thoughtful in your relationship.

- **Do things you don't want to do.** Being in a relationship means that you're part of a unit, and you need to think about that if you really want to keep her as well as keeping her satisfied. It's not always about what you want when you want to inspire her to desire you. Most men don't really want to hold bags while their woman shops. Most men really don't want to listen to them drone on and on about a bad person at work. Most men don't want to take care of a purse dog, but it's about doing something for her because she asked you to. You have to be there for her, and you have to be her support system. Listen to her even if you don't want to. Draw her a bath, or just decide to take her out even if you aren't always feeling up to it.

- **Keep some token gift ideas on hand.** Sometimes you need to give someone a gift to show that you favor them. Is she always asking what time it is? Get her a watch. Does she have neck problems? Grab her a pillow. Just pay attention to what she wants, and it'll help you to get thoughtful gifts that aren't too expensive. It's not about the money that you spend on the gift. It's about the thought that you put into it and making sure that she understands the thought that went into the gift.

- **Write her a note on occasion.** This can also be a text message in this day and age, but it doesn't have to be. After all, most alpha males don't have stationary and scented oils for parchment paper on hand. Most alphas do have something they can write on, and you usually have a phone. So sending a note or a message is still a possibility even if you don't have fancy paper on hand. You don't even need to be overly romantic, but an Alpha male will always think of the needs of his pack, and if she's your girl then she's a part of your pack. You just have to keep that in mind and remember that women love when you just show that you're thinking of them even when they're away from you.

- **Start a ritual every now and then.** This can be as simple as making sure to get her a coffee every Friday morning. It can also be as simple as texting her at a certain time of day. When you start a ritual with her you set the schedule, keeping you in control, while also making sure that she wants you to be there every single day. She should be looking forward to you texting her, calling her, and spending time with her. s

Showing Her You Care

Showing her you care can be simple to big. It's all about what you feel comfortable with, but if you want a girl to feel like you favor her then there is no possible way that you can do this without actually putting in some effort. The amount of effort depends on how far into the relationship you are. At the beginning of a relationship it's a little harder to show someone you care, and the gestures are usually a little bigger. If you want to satisfy a woman in a long term relationship, the gestures can be smaller because you're better at reading one another. You'll find more in the next chapter.

Easy Ways to Show Affection

Sometimes the easiest way is to not have to spend too much money, and even alpha's aren't always loaded with spare cash to throw around. Just because you're an alpha male doesn't mean that you have to spend tons of money on the person that you care about to show her that you actually do care. Here are some ways to show that you care without spending anything at all. Of course, not everything is good for every woman. You'll need to pick and choose what you think is within your capabilities as well as something that the woman you like will actually appreciate.

Create a Card

This isn't too hard is it? You can put pen to paper, and that's all you really need. You can create a card or a love note. Of course, you can buy a card from time to time as well. Did you know that there are 'thinking of you' cards? Most men don't, but you can use them when you feel like it. You can pick them up at almost any grocery store or supermarket as well! Some of these places sell these cards for as little as fifty cents. It's really that cheap to give her something out of the blue that will show that you care. If you're not good with words, the cards can say it for you too!

You don't want to do this often, but occasionally it can matter. Even if you don't want to get her a gift on your first month anniversary, for example, you can still get her a card to remind her that you care. This is especially useful if you aren't able to actually spend the day with her because your work doesn't allow for it or you have prior engagements. Remember that you're an alpha male, so you don't need to get sappy. It can be as simple as "I wish I could spend the day with you, and you should know that you're in my thoughts".

Look Her in the Eye

Never underestimate the power of eye contact, and as an alpha you should already know that. You don't look a wolf in the eyes, right? That's because it's seen as a challenge, but it's different when you're talking to your woman. You already know that when you're talking to the woman you care for that you need to make eye contact. Alpha males are not worried about making eye contact. When you do make eye contact with her it seems like you're really staring into her soul, and if you're confident and meaningful when you do it'll show her everything that you want it to.

Of course, that isn't what I'm talking about right now. You want to actually look in her eyes randomly and tell her something about how much you care for her or appreciate her. Tell her something that's truthful. If you aren't in love yet, then don't pretend you are. Tell her that she looks beautiful, or that you're happy she's around. Just tilt her chin up and have a real moment where you connect with her.

Give a Token of Yours

You'll want to give them a token of something you care about. This can be as simple as one of your favorite sweaters or a CD that you like. Just make sure that when they go home to their apartment, that they have something of yours there as well. This will keep you in their mind. It will also show that you're willing to share your material things to them.

Remember that an Alpha male will share with their mate. You'll find a few ideas below!

- **Favorite Shirt:** If she's staying over and doesn't have something to wear to bed, then try offering her a shirt. Sure! You probably want her to sleep naked, but she'll feel so much better like this, and she'll likely feel more comfortable with you afterwards.

- **Favorite CD:** Or it can be a CD that you just think that she'll really like. Just make sure that there's a connection between you two that can be shared in this CD. Maybe it's a song that you heard while you were spending time together that could be "your song"? It

could be that you just heard
she likes the band too.

- **Decoration:** Maybe you
  have something hanging in
  your house that you think
  she likes? She may be
  caught staring at it, such as
  a cool dragon figurine. Try
  giving it to her if you're
  serious about her or if you
  don't' care too much either
  way about the item.
- **Garden Flower:** Is there a
  garden flower that you have
  growing that you can clip and
  bring inside to her? That's
  usually enough to make a girl
  happy. There's no reason
  that you need to buy her a
  whole bouquet.
- **Space:** Give her a little bit of
  space in your home if you
  aren't living together. If she's
  over often and you eat
  together, then just tell her
  that she can help you
  grocery shop and bring some

groceries to put there. If she stays over a lot, then clear a drawer so that she can keep some things over at your place. You'd be surprised how much this will mean to your woman.

Say Thank You

If they've done something for you, you shouldn't feel bad about thanking them for it. This is best when done in person. That way you can squeeze their hand and look them in the eye when you say thank you. It will make her feel like you really mean it. Most women feel underappreciated by friends and family far too often. Of course, some don't even realize that they feel that way. it goes a long ways to satisfying a woman outside of the bedroom to make sure that she realizes how much of a difference that she makes in your life. If she helps you out by giving you a place to feel safe? Tell her that. If she makes you feel great after sex? Tell her that. If she enriches your life by making you try new things? Thank her for that. It's all really that simple in saying thank you and showing her appreciation.

Cook Them Dinner

Do you live together? No, well you don't need to worry about that too much. If you don't live together yet, then ask if they will come over to your place so that you can cook them dinner. You can also ask to go over to their place. If you take them into your place, then you'll be able to take control of the situation because it is your space. There's always an option, and remember that an alpha male is nothing if not adaptable. If you feel that it's best to go over to her place, then it shows that you are comfortable even in new environments. It'll even show that you're comfortable with her.

Offer them Your Skill

Everyone has a skill, and when you offer yours to her she feels like you care about her. It may be building a website, teaching her how to fish, showing her how to bowl. It doesn't matter if it's some minor repair work or even just baking for her. Offer her something that you're good at that can help her or spoil her. Below you'll find a few things that most men can help with that women need.

- Their yard may need cut.
- There may be a squeaky door that's hard to close.
- Maybe she needs her porch boards replaced.
- Sometimes women need help cleaning the gutters.

- Some women need help with eating healthier.
- Some women need help grocery shopping because they can't lift everything.
- Some women need help repairing a leak that they have somewhere.

Take Photos

Take photos of things that you want to share with them or just photos of you two together. These photos can be important to her just as much as it is important to you. Make sure that you appear comfortable to take photos together, which will also show that you're confident in your appearance. Taking photos will also help to make her feel beautiful. If a picture doesn't turn out the way that she wants, tell her that you can delete it but that you find her beautiful in it anyways.

Cementing Your Place in Her Life

You know that the woman in your life needs you to favor her. Of course, it goes beyond that. You want to cement your place in her life. You want to make her remember you. You want to create a connection that won't easily be forgotten. You want her to think of you and think of good things, and that's exactly what this chapter is about.

Ask Interesting Questions

You already know that communication is important in any relationship. Of course, you'll find that even when you're trying to start one you'll need to ask both intimate and interesting questions. Learn to ask interesting questions about what's going on in her life.

This will be a little more romantic, and it'll make her take an active interest in you since you're taking an active interest in her. You don't want to sit back and ask the old questions that everyone asks.

Figure out what she's passionate about as well as interested in. don't just ask the questions either. You need to follow up on what she tells you as well. If she tells you about an issue that she's dealing with emotionally, health wise, at work, or even with family, you'll want to ask her how she's dealing with it as well. Make sure to go the extra mile, and don't forget to see if you can assist her as well. People will always be drawn to people that take a sincere interest in you. Women want someone that is willing to listen to their daily struggles. Below you'll find a few interesting questions that you can ask.

- "What does your day usually look like?"
- "What's your favorite hobby? A girl like you must be pretty talented."
- "So you don't seem the type to just stay at home, where would you like to go if you could go anywhere in the world?"
- "What's the best compliment that you've ever received? I'm sure you've received many."
- "How do you get along with your family? I always found it to be rather important."
- "Who inspires you? Do you want to be like anyone?"
- "Is there any place in this town that you absolutely love?"
- "Was there a place that you lived before? Did you love it more?"
- "Do you view the glass half empty or half full? Or do you

just think that it's malformed?"

- "What's the strangest thing you've ever done? We all have a good story or two. I could tell you a few of mine, but only if you tell me yours."
- "What do you value most in the relationship? I like it when my pretty girls are honest. Can you be?"

Publically Praise Her

This is a simple way to be more romantic and forge a connection. Praising a woman makes her look up to you as someone who cares about her. Once the connection to you and praise is formed it's not easily broken. Women need to be celebrated, and when you praise her publically that's exactly what you're doing.

You need to give her sincere praise as well as adoration when in the company of others to build a solid foundation of both trust and gratitude. It can be easy to criticize others as well as complain about others. Try something different, and that will help to build a proper relationship. Talk about how your girlfriend excels. Talk about what you like about her, and say it not just to her. Say it to the people around you in front of her. Doing this will build up her feminine confidence, and it shows that you're compassionate and caring.

It will also build up her trust in you and how loyal you are to her. It shows that you won't go searching for someone else, which will in turn remind her that she should be loyal to you. It'll also help to build up her self-worth, so make sure to give her encouragement and be her source of inspiration. If she has self-worth, then she isn't going to be looking for other people that can make her feel that high. You'll be living her that high, and the more self-worth she has the less work you'll have to do in the long run. Now, you don't always want to just compliment her eyes or her clothing. You'll want to have unique compliments, so keep in mind some of the compliments below.

- "Even after so long, you continue to surprise me."
- "Your personality always seems to brighten my day."
- "I dream about you, you know."
- "I don't think that I'll ever get enough of you."
- "You're smarter than people give you credit for."
- "You have more potential than you know. It's okay. I know it."
- "Spending time with you makes me happy."
- "You don't ever need to change anything. Well,

maybe you could depend on
me more."

- "I enjoy spending time with
you, and I love how your
mind works."

Expressing Your Feelings

Men have emotions to, and we
both know that it's true. Stop
trying to fake that you don't have
them for some misguided
masculinity. Alpha males can
express their feelings contrary to
popular belief. Your girlfriend
doesn't always want you to be
mysterious. Sometimes they want
you to be open and honest, but
this doesn't mean that you have to
go on and on.

It doesn't mean that you have to
sit there and ply her with pretty
words to assure her that you love
her. It doesn't mean that you have
to complain about your day or
make your emotions to blatantly

obvious. It just means that you need to be careful to make her feel appreciated. When you're upset, don't hide it. An alpha male doesn't have to hide anything because they're comfortable in their own skin. Enjoy wildflowers through hiking, the beach or even the park. Not only is this a nice outing, but it'll reveal a slightly more sensitive nature.

Making her Remember

As an alpha male you should be sure that she wants you, but you want to keep her wanting you. You already know that starting a ritual can do that because she remembers you. However, you need to make sure that she's thinking about you often. Tokens of affection a help with this as well. Below you'll find a few ways to make sure she remembers and misses you.

- **Songs:** Send her a song that you label as yours. This way when she misses you or thinks about you she will have the urge to play it.
- **Chores:** Do the least favorite chore. This is another way to show that you favor her. Of course, this is most likely a manly chore anyways. Women don't like cutting the grass or taking out the trash. Of course, depending on the woman it could also be doing the dishes. Try to make sure that it's a chore you're okay doing because she usually has a few she doesn't want to have to do.
- **Time:** Insert yourself into her life. So many people think that an alpha male has to be mysterious, and that can be a good thing. However, if you insert yourself into her daily life

then she'll want to see more of you as well.

- **Distance:** Don't blow up her phone. Remember that inserting yourself into her life doesn't mean that you should just blow up her phone again and again. Sometimes all you need to do is give her a little space so that she wants to see you in person.

The 2nd F: Feeding Her

This may seem a bit odd, but you need to feed her. Meals are an intimate time to share with someone, and you want to share this time with a woman that you're trying to make a real and long lasting connection with. Eating tells you a lot about someone, and it's more than a preference in food that you'll learn by eating with a woman you care for. Think about it, she eats every single day, and you want to be able to spend that time with her if you want the relationship to work.

You will satisfy her if you take care of this need as well. This is a basic need that will need to be met, and it's one that you can fulfil continuously. This doesn't mean that you need to feed her every meal every day. It does mean that you'll want to make a conscious effort to have a meal with her at least once a week.

Why Eating Together Matters

Before you realize the importance of feeding her, you can understand why it's important that you feed her if you want to satisfy her.

- **No Food Shaming:** You don't want to be with a girl that tries to change your eating habits. You're an alpha male, and you don't need to change your habits to suit her. You want someone that likes at least somewhat the same food that you do. You also want to show that you won't shame her for the food that she eats.
- **Conversation:** When you feed her, it's going to be a conversation. It doesn't matter if you're buying

something for her, taking her out to dinner, or if you're cooking for her. You'll still have time to actually talk face to face with her, which women find very satisfying.

- **Sharing:** You want to show your woman that you're more than capable of sharing with her, and this includes sharing your food and your time.

Cooking as an Alpha

Every alpha male should know how to cook because it's important to know that you can take care of yourself. A woman will want to take care of you because you want her to. She doesn't want you to have to need to take care of her. In the next chapter you'll learn a little more about what recipes you can cook for her to really impress her without too much trouble, but there are a few things you need to do while you cook that will make the difference. Just follow the list below.

- **Talk:** You'll want to actually talk while you're cooking dinner unless you're trying to surprise her. If she isn't there, then try to send a picture of the ingredients with a playful text.
- **Make Choices:** When you're cooking for her, you'll either need to make the choices for her. This is sometimes the best thing to do, but there are times that you'll want her input and opinion.
- **Atmosphere:** You'll need to keep a light atmosphere as well. You will need to use your social skills as an alpha male to make it an enjoyable experience and not a boring one. You shouldn't ever let sharing a meal or even meal prep be boring.

Taking Her Out

You don't always need to cook. Feeding her can be as simple as a date night. You can take her out, but remember that you'll want that to have arrange. It should range from casual to romantic. It all depends on the day, and you should always indulge in a little bit of both. Keep in mind that if you can agree on a restaurant you can agree on anything.

Now, since you're an alpha male, you'll actually want to pick the restaurant most of the time. It can be the hardest thing for a woman to decide what restaurant she wants to go to. So try to take the lead, and it'll help to take the pressure off of her most of the time. Below you'll find what you need in order to be an alpha male and satisfy here while taking her out to a restaurant.

- **Pick the Place:** Picking the place will help to relieve the pressure from her. Of course, you'll want to let her help sometimes, but you shouldn't feel bad about taking control of the situation. Just make sure that you know there's at least something on the menu you think she will like as well. Never pic the place strictly because you like it without regards to if she will or not.
- **Help to Order:** Sometimes a woman doesn't want to have to order all on her own. It can be difficult, and it can seem like too many choices. Make some suggestions, or just ask outright if it would be okay if you order for her. If you just do it without asking it can be slightly offensive, so make sure that you're careful while still being assertive.

- **Direct on a Dress code:**
  Don't assume that she knows
  to dress fancy just because
  you picked a fancy
  restaurant. Did you tell her
  that you picked one? Does
  she directly know that you'll
  be dressing up? Did you give
  her enough time to get
  dressed up? Are you going
  somewhere that is hard to
  navigate? Is it a pier or has a
  gravel driveway? If so, you
  might want to tell her to
  wear flats. If you really want
  to score some extra brownie
  points, try buying her that
  new dress that you want her
  to wear. It'll help her to get
  into something a little more
  daring than she's
  comfortable with if you want
  to see her in it as well,
  especially if you pay for it!
- **Always Dress Nice:** It
  doesn't matter if it's a first
  date or if you've been

together for years. If you're going out with her, make sure that you dress nice. This doesn't always mean that you need to be in a button up, but make sure that you've showered and shaven if you shave. Mae sure you ran a comb through your hair, and make sure that it doesn't look like you pulled your clothes out of the dirty clothes pile and did a 'sniff check'.

More than a Meal

It can be more than a meal, and I'm not just talking about the experience. You'll find that it can be more than just something you cook for her. It can be a treat as well. Get her that cupcake or muffin while you're at the bakery. Get her coffee in the morning if you know she drinks it. Pick up some tea at the store if you know she drinks tea. You don't even have to go out of your way to do it. You can simply wait until you're on your next grocery run. Try some of these treats to show her that you care and get her hooked by making her know that you're thinking about her.

- **Unusual Candies:** Try something that she hasn't had before. Is there that candy from a different region? Something new that came out that you want to show her? Try that local bakery and try a new unusual candy or sweet together, and that will actually go even further in making her feel like you want to connect with her. Women find that type of connection extremely satisfying both in and outside of the bedroom. If you share things outside of the bedroom, then they'll want to explore and share more inside the bedroom as well.

- **Something Near You Work:** Is there a bakery near you work? Stop there and get her something. Tell her that it was because you wanted to get her something sweet after a long day without her.
- **Coffee & Tea:** Just a single hot beverage can make a difference. Hot beverages are great if you want to share an intimate moment or give her comfort.
- **Groceries:** Sometimes just some extra groceries can help out, especially if you're eating at her place often. For example, if you go to get some fresh vegetables from the farmer's market, then try to get some for her as well.
- **New Foods:** It doesn't have to be sweets. Sometimes

new foods are great too. If you like lamb and she's never had lamb, try to get her lamb kebobs for dinner or take her to a new place.

- **Tip:** Tipping is usually a good thing as well, since it'll show that you actually care about your wait staff. This doesn't mean that you have to tip outrageously or tip if you received horrible service. Just remember that she will judge you on how you treat others.

About Cooking for Her

The first thing you should ask yourself is if you know how to cook? You should know how to feed yourself, but that doesn't mean you can coo well. If you can cook well, then you probably don't need this chapter. Of course, these recipes are actually easy to use, so you may still want to try them from time to time. Of course, there is a shopping section in this chapter that is great for anyone.

Shopping for the Meal

Just because you're an alpha male doesn't mean that you should just go to the store and buy boxed food. You won't impress her with mac and cheese, but you'll find that you don't have to have the most expensive food either. Just wholesome foods and recipes can really make the difference. You'll want to make sure that you buy quality ingredients whenever you can. Below you'll find some shopping tips that will impress a woman and satisfy her when you're feeding her.

- **Shop Fresh:** Sometimes the best way to get qualities ingredients is to shop fresh. Instead of going to a normal grocery store, try going to a butchers for your meat. It is a common misconception that a butcher will be more expensive. Sometimes you'll find that a butcher is actually less expensive because the meat is from around your hometown. You can also get a variety of different meats as well than you'd usually get in a grocery store. You will also want to try to get fresh fruits and vegetables, which will limit you to shopping in season as well. Remember that vegetables and fruits will usually taste better when they're in season as well. The best part is that at a farmer's market, you're likely to get these fruits and vegetables a little cheaper as well since they're also going to be from local sellers. Many flea markets will have a small section for fruits and vegetables too!

- **No Boxes:** I'm not saying this is a golden rule, but it should be a rule that you keep in mind. Why buy boxed mashed potatoes when you can just boil and mash your own? The homemade ones will taste better. Why buy mac and cheese when you can make an easy cheese sauce in under twenty minutes?
- **Try the Recipe:** You'll want to make sure that you try the recipe before you try to cook for someone because it may

need a little bit of tweaking. Tweaking a recipe means that you'll make it your own as well, which is something that you'll be able to boast about when you are cooking it for her.

More about the Meal

You need to think about how you're going to serve the meal as well, and this one is easy. Just don't serve it on paper plates with plastic silverware. You don't have to have the fanciest plates, but make sure that you have plates that match one another. You just need two matching plates. You don't need silver plated silverware, but you do need ones that aren't broken or bent. Silverware sets can be cheap, so just make sure that you have one on hand.

Don't leave excess dishes in the sink either. You will want to clean as you go so that you don't look like a slob. Remember that you're in control of the situation. At least stack the dishes neatly so that they aren't scattered everywhere. If you're in her house, you'll want to take care of the dishes as well. Besides an alpha male doesn't have to make anything a "man's job" and a "woman's job". When you're feeding her, then it's a treat for her. You should treat it that way, which is why you shouldn't always make her do the dishes.

Think about Grilling

Everyone loves a man that can cook, but women love a man that can grill even more. Grilling is consider the manliest form of cooking, so you might want to think about grilling for her. You'll still need to make some side dishes. Below you'll find a few easy grilling combinations, and you can use any pre-made marinade to make your grilling more flavorful as well as quicker.

- Burgers, baked fries made with coconut oil and basil cut from real potatoes, easy corn on the cob which is grilled as well.
- Steak goes great with homemade mashed potatoes, gravy which you can use a packet for, and some blanched green beans cooked that's pan fried with salt and pepper afterwards.
- Chicken skewers goes great with vegetable skewers that have potatoes, zucchini, squash, and onion on them.
- Grilled lamb shoulder blades goes great with baked potatoes and baked Brussel sprouts.
- Grilled pork chops goes great with baked cabbage and pan roasted potatoes.

Roasted Salmon & Crispy Potatoes

You can easily pair this with a salad, and then you'll have everything you need to impress and keep a woman. This is great on a first date or even on a weekend. Most people love salmon, and it doesn't have to be hard to cook. This will also keep you in the "whole foods" section, making it seem like you're at least somewhat health conscious and don't cut corners. Remember that being an alpha means that you're in control of everything you do and that should extend to the kitchen.

Time: 30 Minutes

Serves: 2

Ingredients:

- 1 Medium Lemon, Zested & Juiced

- 8 Basil Leaves, Chopped Fine
- 2 Garlic Cloves, Chopped Fine
- 2 Tarragon Sprigs, Chopped Fine
- 2 Salmon Fillets, 6 Ounces
- ¼ Bunch Flat Leaf Parsley, Chopped Fine
- Sea Salt & Pepper to Taste
- 3 Tablespoons Olive Oil, Extra Virgin & Divided
- 1 ½ Teaspoons Flakey Sea Salt
- 2 lbs Fingerling Potatoes, Halved

Directions:

1. Start by heating your oven to 425.
2. Blend your lemon zest and sea salt together.
3. Toss the potatoes in, and then add black pepper and salt to taste. Drizzle the olive oils over them.

4. Arrange your potatoes in a single layer one prepared baking sheet.
5. Roast your potatoes for twenty-five minutes, and then remove them.
6. Toss with lemon salt again, and return to the oven.
7. Roast for about five minutes more. They should turn a golden brown.
8. While your potatoes are roasting, you'll need to season your salmon fillets with sea salt and your pepper.
9. Mix your basil, garlic. Parsley, remaining olive oil and tarragon together in a bowl.
10. Spread this mixture over your salmon, and place your salmon on a baking dish.
11. Roast until flaky which should take about ten

minutes. Let it rest for ten minutes before serving.

Asparagus & Lemon Pasta

If the girl you are trying to impress is vegetarian or vegan, then you might want to go but of your way to make her something she can eat. This would be a recipe that would be great for a vegan or vegetarian, and you can always cook some baked or grilled chicken for you to put overtop of it as well. Even shrimp goes great on the side.

Time: 30 Minutes

Serves: 2

Ingredients:

- 12 Ounces Asparagus, Trimmed & Washed
- 4 Large Cloves Garlic, Minced
- 4 Tablespoons Cornstarch

- 2 Tablespoons Nutritional Yeast
- 2 ½ Cups Almond Milk, Unsweetened
- 10 Ounces Bow Tie Pasta
- Olive Oil
- 2 Lemons
- Sea Salt & Pepper to Taste

Directions:

1. Start by heating your oven to 400.
2. Place your asparagus on a baking sheet, tossing it in ½ tablespoon of your olive oil. Sprinkle salt and pepper over it, and then top with slices of lemon.
3. Bake for twenty to twenty-five minutes. Remove from the oven, and then chop.
4. Bring a pot of water to boil in the meantime, and salt so that it boils faster.
5. While that' heating heat up a large skillet over medium heat. Once that's hot, add in

three tablespoons of your olive oil and garlic. Whisk together, and cook for about one to two minutes. Your garlic should start to brown.

6. Add in three tablespoons of cornstarch, and continue to whisk. Cook for about thirty seconds, and then whisk in ½ cup of almond milk at a time.

7. Add pasta to your boiling water, cooking as your package instructs. Drain and then set it aside.

8. For an extra creamy sauce, add your sauce to a blender and blend. Add in your nutritional yeast and more salt and pepper. Add another tablespoon of cornstarch, blending until creamy and smooth. Add back to the pan, and cook over medium to medium low heat. Continue to cook until it thickens. Add

the juice of half of your lemon, and then stir.

9. Add ¾ of your chopped asparagus and cooked pasta to your sauce, tossing to coat. Serve warm.

Classic Slow Cooker Pot Roast

This is great if she isn't going to be over while you cook the meal because there isn't anything impressive about a crockpot meal other than the way it tastes. Of course, you'll find that the taste really does make up for the easy way it's cooked, and it's nothing short of impressive. Pot roast is a comfort food as well. You'll even have leftovers so that you can spend less time cooking that week as well!

Time: 5 Hours 15 Minutes

Serves: 4-6

Ingredients:

- 1 Tablespoon + 1 Teaspoon Cornstarch
- 3 Tablespoons Tomato Paste
- 2 Large Carrots, Cut into 2" Pieces
- 1 Medium Onion, Cut into ½" Wedges
- 1 lb Gold Potatoes, Scrubbed & Halved
- 2 Tablespoons Worcestershire Sauce
- ¾ Cup Chicken Broth, Low Sodium
- 3 lbs Beef Roast, Trimmed of Excess Fat
- 4-6 Garlic Cloves, Mashed
- Sea Salt & Pepper to Taste

Directions:

1. You'll need a five to six quart crockpot, and stir in your broth and cornstarch until its smooth. It's best to do this with two tablespoons of broth and cornstarch, whisking together until smooth, and

then whisk it with the rest of the broth.

2. Add in your tomato paste, carrots, onion, Worcestershire sauce, and potatoes. Season with your sea salt and pepper to taste.

3. Season your roast with garlic, pepper and sea salt. Place it on top of your vegetables.

4. Cover and cook on high for about five hours. You can also cook on low for eight hours to make it tenderer.

5. Serve warm.

Drink Can Impress Too!

An alpha male that can make a drink is incredibly sexy and appealing to women. It has to go past being able to pour whiskey over ice cubes. Women like fruity drinks, but that doesn't mean that you have to drink them too. What you drink is completely up to you, but as an alpha male you should feel comfortable in your masculinity to drink whatever you'd like to.

Not only making drinks can impress her, but you'll want to know what drinks to order as well. We'll cover everything you need to know about alcoholic beverages and how they can impress her in this chapter. Of course, it's important to have nonalcoholic refreshments on hand as well when she comes to visit you!

Ordering to Impress

Alpha males should be comfortable enough with their own masculinity to order whatever they like, but a woman does appreciate a man that can order a manly drink. if you're just starting to go out with a woman or if you're trying to pick her up at the bar, ordering the best drink is the first step to impressing and satisfying the woman you want to keep. Below you'll find a few drinks and why you shoulder order them.

- **Bloody Bull:** It's a version of a Bloody Mary, and it's made with vodka, Worcestershire sauce, Tabasco, and a beef bouillon. It sounds impressive, and it looks like a manly drink.
- **Tom Collins:** This is a traditionally manly drink that's even named after a man. It's made from lemon

juice, sugar, club soda, ice, and gin.

- **Whiskey Sour:** This is a drink that is made from white egg, sugar, lemon juice and bourbon. With the egg white it may be called a Boston Sour depending on where you go.

Make it to Impress

Here you'll find a few easy drinks that you can make at home to impress her. Though, a bottle of wine can usually work as well. Just make sure that you don't buy a cheap bottle that you know nothing about. At least look up a little bit before you buy it or get a suggestion. Just remember that when you have her there with you in your house, then you are responsible for her safety. Don't rush the situation if she doesn't want it, and be a gentlemen if you need to. You're an alpha male, and that means that you aren't desperate for sex. You can get sex whenever you want, but if you want to satisfy a girl make sure that you have sex at the right time. This will be explained more in a later chapter.

Sea breeze

Vodka is easy to get, and so are the rest of the ingredients in this easy to make cocktail. Just remember that grapefruit juice can interfere with most birth control, so ask her if it's okay before you make it.

Recipe

- 16 Ounces Vodka
- 30 Ounces Cranberry Juice
- 12 Ounces White Grapefruit Juice
- Lime Wedges to Garnish
- Ice

Strawberry Lemonade Sparkler

This is a pink and girly drink that is easy to make, and it'll show that you really took the time to think about her. It's easy to keep everything on hand to make this drink as well.

Recipe:

- 4 Ounces Strawberry Vodka
- 4 Ounces Pink Lemonade
- 4 Ounces Sparkling Wine
- Fresh Mint & Strawberries to Garnish

Easy Frozen Peach Bellini

This easy recipe only requires two ingredients, and you can get the frozen peaches in the frozen section of your grocery store. You just need to blend them first and then mix in your sparkling wine. It's easy, and

Recipe:

- ½ Cup Frozen Peaches, Blended into a Puree
- ½ Cup Sparkling Wine

Order It to Impress Her

When you take a girl out, you can always let her order for herself. Of course, this usually isn't the alpha male way. It impresses a girl when you order for her, or if you just meet her at the bar and send a drink to her. This only works if you know what type of drink to order her, which is what this section is all about.

- **Gin & Tonic:** if she isn't a whiskey drinker, it's okay. The chances are high that she'll like a gin and tonic. It's a classic drink that screams elegance, and ordering it makes you seem like an old fashion gentlemen which women find very satisfying.

- **Bellini:** Ordering a Bellini, especially a peach Bellini, will help to show her that you're catering to her feminine side and you want her to enjoy the night.
- **White Russian:** This is a sweet and creamy cocktail that will help to make sure that you impress her. It's the perfect cocktail for after dinner as well.

The 3rd F: Fuck Her

This may seem a little crude, but it's something that you shouldn't be shy about talking about or doing. Every relationship has sex in it if it's a healthy one. It's normal to want to sexually satisfy the woman you're with, and you need to know how to do it. There is a thin line between being sexually assertive and sexually aggressive though, and that's the first thing that you need to learn.

Being Sexually Assertive

You need to understand that being sexually assertive would mean that you're telling her when you want to have sex. You will want to tell her when you expect sex. Don't try to give hints, but do try to have some foreplay. Remember that you want to be a generous lover if you want to satisfy a woman. However, being sexually aggressive is trying to insist on sex before someone is ready. You can be sexually aggressive, which is a no-no, and still not rape someone. Sexually aggressive is just wrong, and it'll make a woman want to leave you, doing the exact opposite of satisfying her.

The Elements of Good Sex

Good sex isn't just about rutting in the bedroom and going for as long as possible. Being an alpha male means that you need to bring more than that to the bedroom. You'll find everything you need to know to provide a great sexual experience for her below.

- **Being Present:** You need to be completely immersed in the moment. It requires you and your partner to be this way, which means you'll need to engage her completely. They should never be allowed to disengage long enough to judge or citizen their actions. They shouldn't get distracted or groggy, which is why alcohol can actually hamper a sexual experience. You'll also want to make sure that you aren't distracted when having sex as well. This will create transcendent sex where you can forget about everything besides the "now" and the "us".

- **Being in Sync:** You need a real foundation if you want extraordinary flex. You need a strong connection or you will not be able to achieve transcendent sex. This is why you don't want to rush sex so that you can have this when you finally do engage with each other.
- **Communication:** Great sex requires communication and

attentiveness. You need to open about your desires, which will in turn allow her to be open about her desires as well. Don't be afraid to tell her what you want, and make sure that she isn't afraid to express her like or dislike for things as well. You need to be alert when it comes to your partner's reactions as well. You need to speak only about the truth when it comes to this as well. Show what you fee and don't be embarrassed, guilty or ashamed. Great sex is creative, generous, transcendent and liberating.

- **Exploration:** Great sex should be a journey. You shouldn't be afraid to have fun and take risks. Take it on a challenge to find what each other enjoys, and feel free to explore your instincts and natural curiosity. You

shouldn't be afraid to laugh
and enjoy sex even as it gets
messy and you experience a
few hiccups along the way.

- **Surrender:** It doesn't matter
  if she's giving into your
  desires or if you're giving
  into your own. You both need
  to surrender to pleasures
  that you're enjoying. Sex is
  an event that is meant to be
  enjoyed and experienced.

How Often

You may be asking yourself how
often you should be having sex.
The answer is pretty simple. You
should be having sex as often as
you and she want sex. There
should be no shame in sharing
your bodies with each other, and
as an alpha male it is your job to
make sure that she understand
that. Women have related
emotions to sex and most of the

time due to social concepts women relate it to shame. They don't want to want sex. However, women usually have just as high of a sex drive as men.

You need to appreciate her, making sure that she realizes you don't think she's a slut or whore just because they want to have sex. If you can make her feel like sex isn't shameful, then you'll find women will even tell you if they want sex more often, want something particular, or just feel that they want to change something in the bedroom. Now, this doesn't mean that you can't talk dirty to her. Many women like this, and if she does then you can say whatever you both agree on in the bedroom.

The difference would be that afterwards and outside of sex you'll need to treat her like she's the only thing that matters to you. Respect her, love her, and take care of her.

Women need emotional connections, and this is called aftercare. If you have a particularly rough and dirty sex scene, you'll want to take care of her emotions afterwards. This can include cuddling her, getting her something to drink, or just something as simple as telling her that you love her and appreciate her. Anything to erase the shame she might feel from letting go and enjoying all of the names you called her and everything that you just did together and shared.

When Aggression is OK

Romantic aggression is okay, but you need to make sure that the person you're into is into that. Of course, if you are then you need to find a woman that is okay with that as well. if you aren't sure how to start, then try with a little hair tugging as she gets up from the bed or when you're about to get busy. Some girls even like choking, but you should never start with this unless you already know that she's interested in it. Spanking is another great warmup for many women, and it'll surprise you how many women actually like this.

To satisfy women, you may actually want to let her take the lead from time to time as well. Women are told that they should be the docile ones in bed, but many women would love to experiment with having the upper hand. Let her play the role of aggressor, and she might like it. Never do this just to satisfy her though. You're an alpha male and you shouldn't ever do something that you don't want to, especially in the bedroom.

Dirty Talk to Please Her

Many women actually like it when you talk dirty to them. Of course, not all dirty talk has to be degrading. You'll learn a lot about dirty talk and what you can and can't say in this section. Dirty talk also helps to make sure that you engage her mentally just as you engage her physically, which will lead to her satisfaction.

Just remember that it isn't always about what you say. Sometimes it's about how you say it. Make sure that you don't rush your words. As an alpha male you already know that you should talk with intent, making sure it's slow and pronounced carefully. Remember that women love a husky voice, so let your emotion and tone show through with your words as well.

All about the When

The first thing you should know about dirty talk is what that it starts before you actually start having sex. Just start with being honest. Tell them what you want to do with them or to them before you begin, and that's the best warm up. Tell them what you like about doing it, what you want to do, what you're going to ask them to do, and so on. You need to just open up about what you desire.

Remember that alpha males are confident in their own desires, and so you need to show that confidence in yourself. This works best when it's in person, but you can send ad dirty text to get their engine revved up and ready for you the moment you get home or to their place as well. Tell them what you liked doing to them and what you're thinking about. You can talk about past experiences. You'll want to give your partner feedback as you have sex with them as well. Encourage them to do what it is that you are enjoying.

Description is Key

Description is also key to good dirty talk. There is nothing wrong with "I love your body" or "just like that baby", but it isn't descriptive. It is dirty talk, but it's a much milder form than what will really satisfy her. for example instead of telling them "yeah just like that", try telling them "Yeah just like that baby I love when your pretty little mouth wraps around my cock. Take it deeper. Good girl, you sexy little slut". The last one is going to get her much more excited about what you're saying, and you'll likely notice a difference in her enthusiasm as well.

Use Your Senses

Dirty talk isn't just about what you can see. It's also about what you can taste and smell and touch. You have to love more than the sight of her. You might love the sounds that she make. You might love the taste of her lips. You might love the way her hair feels when you're pulling her head up and down as she blows you. You will want to talk about it all.

Figure out Profanity

Some women really get off on profanity but not all of them do. Remember that even though you're the alpha, an alpha caters to the needs of their partner. Even if you're used to using profanity in bed, ask yourself if it's essential that you keep using it. If it isn't, then you might want to cut down so that your partner doesn't get turned off because of excessive use of profanity.

Beginner Dirty Talk

You should know what beginner dirty talk is, and you'll find it here. This serves as a guide on how to start if you haven't talked dirty before. It will also show you what to avoid if you want to up your game.

- "That feels amazing."
- "Tell me when you're going to come."
- "I love the way you look at me when you want sex."
- "Come here and ride me."
- "I love the sounds you make."
- "I love the way you're wet for me."
- "You're making me hard."

Intermediate Dirty Talk

With a little bit of practice you'll want to move to intermediate dirty talk. That's what this section is about. Just get creative, but you'll see that there are a few examples below.

- "I want you on your knees."
- "Let's fuck in front of the mirror so you can see the same desire in your eyes I do."
- "You have such a perfect pussy, and I want to use it right now."
- "You look so sexy right now with your hair like that."
- "You belong to me just as much as I do you."

Advanced Dirty Talk

These aren't for the faint of heart, and you'll find that advanced dirty talk will have her addicted to you.

Just make sure that she's into words like "slut" and some swearing before you use it.

- "You're a dirty little slut, but you're my slut. You know that, don't out?"
- "I want you to gag on my cock as you taste me."
- "You have such a pretty little face, and you deserve to be fucked."
- "I want to fuck you until the sun starts to rise."
- "Tell me who owns this perfect body of yours?"

Bonus Banter Cheat Sheet

It doesn't matter if you're in a long term relationship or if you're just getting one started. You still need to know some funny banter that goes beyond just the average pickup line. It helps to break tense situations, awkward days and even boring ones.

Beginning relationship

This banter will help you to banter when you first meet someone or are still in the beginning of your relationship with the person.

- I said I wasn't going to date a bad girl again. You should get out of here.
- No, no. it's okay. You don't need to buy me a drink.
- You seem almost safe.

- I can tell you don't like me. Not as a friend at least.
- It's not going to work out. I wouldn't take your crap, and you wouldn't take mine either.

Long Term Relationship

This banter can be used in a long term relationship after a fight, on a date night, or just during a boring night.

- If you kiss me on the cheek, I might let you forgive me.
- I'm just too high maintenance for you.
- You don't have to be nervous, but it's just too cute.
- I'm not a sausage on feet!
- You've lost me. I can't talk to you for two minutes. Time out for you.
- Here's another chance for you to compliment me.

Conclusion

Now you know everything you need to in order to fully satisfy a woman. We've went over the 3 F's to get her and keep her, satisfying her every need. You favor her, feed her and fuck her until she's head over heels for the alpha male that you are. You know what to order to impress her, what to do to impress her, and how to care for her in all of the ways you need to both in and out of the bedroom. Once you find a girl you want, there's no reason to let her get away when you have this handy guidebook. All that's left is putting what you've learned into practice.